I Love You Now and I Loved You Then

An adoption love story from the
I Knew You Before You Were Born series

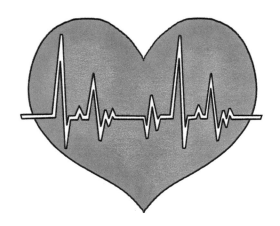

Written by Becki Carter

Illustrated By Valerie Bouthyette

Fulton Books, Inc.
Meadville, PA

Published by Fulton Books 2021

ISBN 978-1-63860-002-2 (paperback)
ISBN 978-1-63860-003-9 (digital)

Printed in the United States of America

To Gabriellah, Christian, Margarita and Isabelle—my four beautiful examples of selfless love!

And to Ray—the one who inspires me to follow my dreams!

"Mama bear, can we read my story again?" asked Baby Hare.

"Of course, Baby Hare," answered Mama Bear. Baby Hare crawled up onto Mama Bear's lap, and Mama began reading.

1

"It all started with your beating heart...ba-bum, ba-bum, ba-bum."

3

"Dear Baby Hare! You became my baby as soon as I saw your little heart beating. Even though you were as tiny as a grain of rice, you have always been a precious life! I love you now and I loved you then!"

Giggling, Baby Hare asked, "How could I have been so small and still be me?"

Mama Bear answered, "We all start our life journey smaller than our own eyes can see, but we have everything within us to become who we are today! Even though you started out tiny, you were mighty!"

"Wow! I was strong?" Delighted, Baby Hare flexing her muscles. "Read me more!"

10

Mama Bear continued.

11

"Although I loved you as much as a mama could, I was not ready to be a mommy. I was scared. I couldn't take care of you and had to make the very hard decision to find a mommy who could give you everything you needed. I love you now AND I loved you then!"

Baby Hare sadly asked, "Why couldn't my mommy take care of me if I came from her tummy?"

"That's a very good question," explained Mama Bear, snuggling Baby Hare into her fur a bit more. "Your birth mommy took excellent care of you while you grew inside of her.

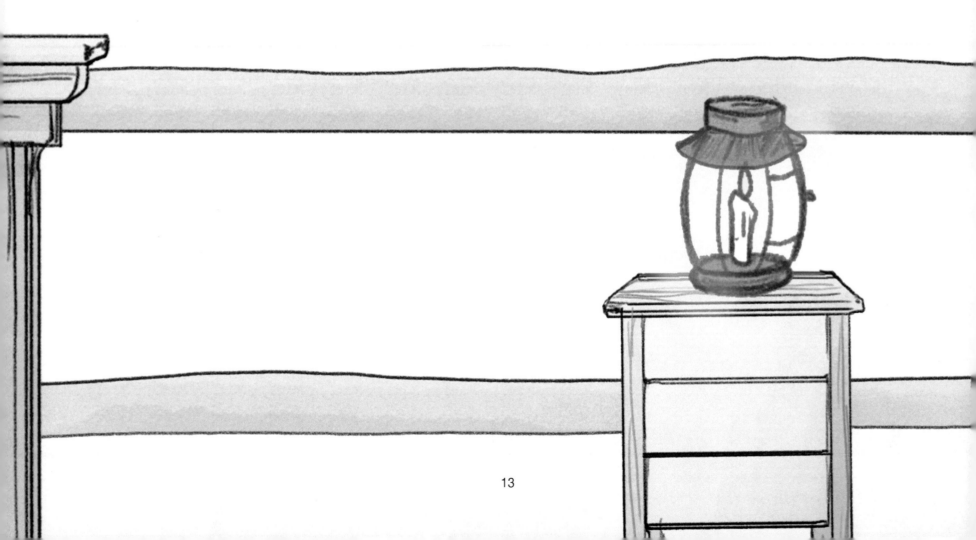

She did everything possible to keep you safe and healthy and wanted to make sure you continued to be safe and healthy after you were born. She loves you now AND she loved you then!"

Baby Hare was excited as Mama Bear continued.

"As you grew, so did my tummy. You quickly became the size of a cherry, an apple, an orange, a banana, and then a coconut until finally, you were a full-sized infant baby! It was time for you to be born!"

Baby Hare quietly said, "This is the happiest and saddest part."
"I know, Baby Hare," said Mama Bear as she continued reading.

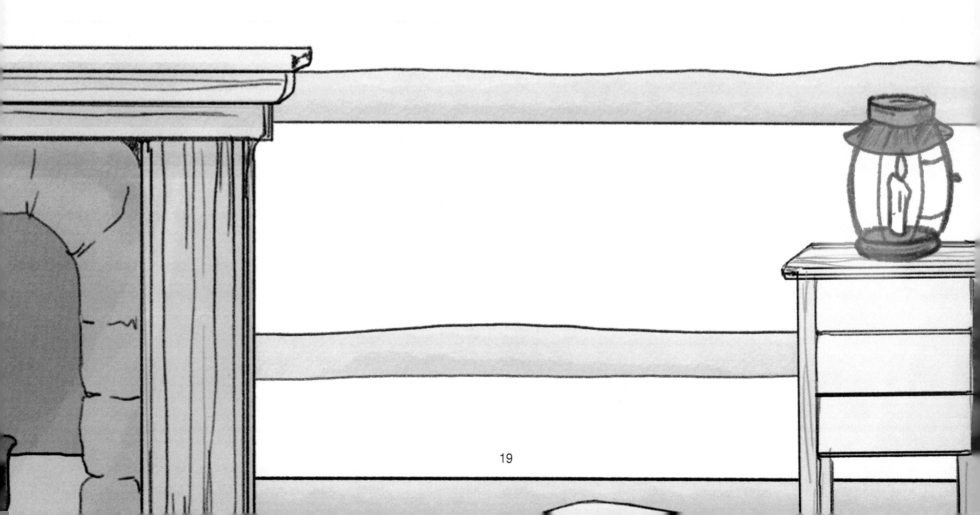

20

"I was so happy to finally see your beautiful face. It was the happiest day of my life. But today I will no longer be your only mommy. Today you will have a new mommy who will take care of you; a mommy who will help you grow, learn, and read you bedtime stories! I love you now AND I loved you then!"

21

22

With wide eyes, Baby Hare said, "I am so lucky to have two mommies. But, Mama, why doesn't everyone have two mommies?"

Mama Bear looked deeply into Baby Hare's eyes and exclaimed, "Oh, Baby Hare! That's because not everyone is as lucky as you!

24

You have two mommies who love
you—the mommy that gave you life

25

and the mommy who gets to share
that life with you every day!

26

We both love you now, we loved you then, AND we'll love you always!"

27

28

Baby Hare snuggled as deeply as possible into Mama Bear's coat, yawned, and drifted off to sleep, feeling very loved.

About the Author

Becki Carter and her three daughters have each been through their own unique adoption experiences and understand first-hand the beautiful and precious gift of adoption. The *I Knew You Before You Were Born* series is not just about their stories, but how families can be changed forever when they open their hearts to this process. They believe in the sanctity of life and that even the smallest of lives matter. They hope your family will be blessed by these stories.

Becki currently resides in Omaha, Nebraska, with her husband Ray; her four children—Gabi, Christian, Mara and Isabelle; her two stepchildren, Jackson and Aidan; and her two grandchildren, Cruz and Malachi.